# The Pension Shield Option™

*Protecting Your Pension,*
*Your Spouse, and Your Legacy*

By George McReynolds, CFP®, CF2® and

Jim Lusk, CFP®, CLU®, ChFC®, CLF®, M.Ed.

Just Abundance Media LLC
Telford, PA

The Pension Shield Option™



First Edition

ISBN 978-1-7372195-3-8

Cover and interior design by: Just Abundance Media LLC

Published by: Just Abundance Media LLC, Telford, PA

Printed in the United States of America

**Disclaimer and Disclosure**

This book is provided for **educational and informational purposes only.** It is not intended to provide, and should not be relied upon as, legal, investment, or tax advice. Every individual's financial situation is unique. Before making any decision regarding your pension, insurance, investments, taxes, or estate plan, you should seek the guidance of a **qualified professional advisor** who is licensed and experienced in those areas. Neither the authors nor the publisher assume responsibility for decisions made without such professional counsel.

**Characters and Examples**

The examples, case files, and characters in this book are used solely for illustration. Some characters are entirely fictitious. Others are drawn from real-world circumstances but have had names, identifying details, and certain facts changed to protect the privacy of individuals and their families. Any resemblance to actual persons, living or deceased, is purely coincidental.

## Dedication

To those who wore the badge, carried the gear, and answered the call.

You stood between order and chaos, between fear and hope, often at great cost.
You've seen things most people can't imagine, and you've done it with courage, grace, and humor.

This book is for you — and for the families who carried the weight right alongside you.
For every spouse who sat up through the long nights.
For every child who waited for the sound of the garage door and exhaled only then.

You've earned more than a pension; you've earned peace.
May these pages help you protect the life you built, the people you love, and the legacy you deserve.

With deep respect and gratitude,

George McReynolds & Jim Lusk

## Contents

# Part I – The Stakes

Chapters 1 to 3

## Introduction

Retirement decisions don't get bigger than this. For public safety professionals, your pension isn't just a paycheck—it's the foundation of your family's future. And at the heart of it lies one question: should you take the maximum pension, or accept a permanent pay cut for the "survivor option"?

Too often, that choice gets made on gut instinct, locker-room advice, or a quick glance at the numbers in your packet. That's a mistake. The truth is, this isn't guesswork. When you run the numbers the right way, the answer becomes clear. The Pension Shield Option™ either works for you—or it doesn't.

That's what makes ignoring it so foolish. You wouldn't go into a fire without checking your gear, or clear a building without backup. Why would you gamble with the single most permanent financial decision of your life without knowing if a smarter option exists?

On most pension election forms, you'll see three boxes to choose from:

- **Option #1:** The Single Life Annuity — the biggest paycheck while you're alive, but it stops the moment you do.
- **Option #2:** The 50% Joint and Survivor Annuity — a permanent pay cut so your spouse gets half your pension if you go first.
- **Option #3:** The 100% Joint and Survivor Annuity — an even bigger cut so your spouse gets the same amount for life.

And then there's what we call **The Pension Shield Option™.**

**The Pension Shield Option™** isn't on your form, but it should be. It's a smarter design: take the maximum pension (Option #1) and redirect part of that extra income into private protection for your spouse and your legacy. If you qualify, especially if you start early, The Pension Shield Option™ can often give you higher net income while alive, tax-free protection for your spouse, and wealth that passes to your children instead of disappearing back into the pension fund.

The chapters ahead will show you how to test this strategy against your own pension, your own health, and your own goals. If the numbers prove it out, the Shield can protect your spouse, preserve your income, and pass on a legacy. If not, you'll know before you sign. Either way, you'll have clarity. And that's the point—**to have clarity, confidence, and control.**

## Chapter 1 – The Retirement Crossroads

Retirement is supposed to be the reward at the end of years of service — a time to finally exhale, enjoy family, and reflect on a career of sacrifice. For public safety employees, however, the transition is rarely simple. Your pension isn't just a paycheck; it's the lifeline that will carry you and your family through the rest of your life. And the decision you make about how to take it is one of the most permanent, consequential financial choices you will ever face.

Most public safety retirees face the same fork in the road:
• Take the maximum monthly pension — the largest possible income during your life — but risk leaving your spouse unprotected; or
• Take the reduced survivor option — accept less income every month for as long as you live, so your spouse has continuing income if you die first.

It sounds straightforward. It isn't. What looks like a simple checkbox in your retirement packet is actually a six-figure decision with long-term consequences.

### The High Stakes of Public Safety Pensions

• Many police officers, firefighters, and EMTs do not receive Social Security benefits. That means the pension is often the only guaranteed lifetime income stream.
• Cost-of-living adjustments (COLA) vary widely between plans. Some include automatic inflation

adjustments, others don't.

• Survivor options almost always come with a permanent reduction in benefits, no matter how long you and your spouse live. There is typically no refund, no cash value, and no chance to reclaim what you gave up.

"What looks like a simple checkbox on your pension form is often the single biggest financial decision of your life."

### The Lesson of Sergeant Rick O'Shea

One of my early police mentors—let's call him Rick O'Shea,—was a legend in the department. Everyone knew him. Respected him. Learned from him. He was old-school tough: worked through injuries, pulled double shifts, trained half the department, and didn't take grief from anyone—especially not politicians.

When Rick retired, he took the single life annuity—the highest monthly payout, but the one that ends when you do.

At the time, he was also subject to the Windfall Elimination Provision (WEP)—the old Social Security penalty that cut earned benefits for people with a government pension. His stay-at-home wife had no pension of her own and not enough work history to qualify for full Social Security on her own record.

When Sergeant Rick passed, everything stopped.

No survivor pension. No Social Security. Just a widow. Alone. With bills. And heartbreak.

Congress finally repealed WEP and GPO in 2025—but the change came too late for her. And for too many like her.

Rick wasn't selfish. He was certainly un-realistic. He just thought he'd live forever. **But your pension decision isn't about betting on your lifespan. It's about protecting theirs.**

### Your Compressed Retirement Timeline

While most civilians retire in their mid-60s, first responders often retire in their 40s or early 50s. Not because they want to—but because their bodies (or minds) demand it.

That early retirement age sounds like a luxury. But it isn't—because it comes with a hidden cost: **your money needs to last a lot longer**, and you may be responsible for covering 10 to 15 years of health insurance before Medicare kicks in.

When you retire early, time stops working for you—and starts working against you.

### The Price of Service: Why Pension Planning Can't Wait

As to the question of *"How long will you live?"* The correct answer is ***"EVERYDAY!"***

Let's be real. Nobody signs up for the job of firefighter, cop, or medic expecting it to be easy. But here's what too many don't expect:

**The life expectancy of a first responder is up to 20 years shorter than the general public.**

Read that again.

### Health: The Silent X-Factor

Shift work. Adrenaline. Trauma scenes. Constant hyper-vigilance. These take a toll that spreadsheets can't measure.

If you pushed a patrol car on rotating shifts for 20 years and got clobbered in a hundred street fights or showed up at too many HazMat scenes or toted too many obese patients down the stairs and then up on to the ambulance you are probably affected by heart disease, PTSD, back injuries, and sleep disorders. These are more common among first responders than almost any other profession. And these don't just affect your quality of life—they impact your longevity and your healthcare costs.

While the average American might live well into their 80s, studies show that many police and firefighters don't make it nearly that far. In fact:

- A National Institutes of Health study found **the average life expectancy of a police officer is just 57 years old**.
- Between the heart strain, toxic exposure, and chronic stress, **the risk of dying from a heart attack between ages 55 and 60 is 35 times higher** than the general public.
- And tragically, **first responders are more likely to die by suicide than in the line of duty.**

This isn't fearmongering. It's the hard truth. And it's why ***your retirement plan isn't just about living well. It's about making sure you get to live at all—and on your terms.***

It's worth noting that other peer-reviewed studies have challenged these findings, indicating that the issue is still debated within the research community.

**What does this mean for you?**
Don't wait for "someday" to figure out your financial future. Make your money work for *you* while you still have the strength, freedom, and time to enjoy it. Because you've already paid the price—in sweat, trauma, and time away from family.

There is a flip side that impacts both your life expectancy and health care costs. If you've been on a fast track for promotion, have attended the FBI National Academy or the National Fire Academy -Fire or EMS Leadership

Track and have kept in good shape physically with a waist under 40" and are financially secure, your picture looks quite different. Studies in both the US and England have found that *"successful people" live up to 10 or more years longer* than "unsuccessful people."

### Success Really *Is* a Matter of Life and Death

**What if we told you that smart financial planning could actually *add years* to your life?**
Turns out, it's not just your wallet that benefits from financial stability—your body does, too.

Multiple studies show that successful people—especially those with higher wealth, education, or socioeconomic status—live significantly longer than those with fewer resources. In fact:

- **Top 10% earners in the U.S. live up to 14 years longer** than those in the bottom 10%, according to research in *JAMA Internal Medicine*.
- A *University College London* study found the wealthiest live **8 to 9 more years free from disability** than the poorest.
- The legendary *Whitehall Studies* proved that **higher job rank alone** correlated with **significantly lower death rates**, even after adjusting for lifestyle and health risks.

Why does wealth—or more broadly, *successful life planning*—have such a profound impact?

Here are the real facts:

- **Better Healthcare Access**: Those with resources get faster, more consistent care.
- **Healthier Lifestyles**: Affluence often means more time, money, and access to stay active and eat well.
- **Less Stress**: Financial security literally reduces stress hormones that wear down your body over time.
- **Stronger Support Systems**: Successful people often have broader, more dependable social networks—another proven contributor to longer life.

Now, we're not saying money buys happiness (although it *does* rent a pretty nice life)—but we are saying this:

**The choices you make now—not just about money, but about clarity, confidence and control —can directly affect how long and how well you live.**

That's why this book isn't just about retirement income—it's about *retirement resilience*. It's your blueprint to living longer, stronger, and with more dignity and options. Which, let's be honest, is the most badass retirement plan of all.

## A Case from the Field

Take the example of a retiring firefighter, Battalion Chief Les Sparks, with 30 years of service and a final average salary of $90,000. His maximum monthly benefit might be $5,000. The 100% survivor option could reduce that to $4,000 a month — permanently. If he and his spouse both live another 25 years, that $1,000 reduction amounts to roughly $300,000 in lost lifetime income. If his spouse dies first, the reduction continues. Nothing is refunded. The pension fund keeps the difference.

### *One Choice, Lifetime Consequences*

- The survivor option may feel like the "safe" bet, but it's irreversible.
- Once you elect it, you are locked in. No second chance if circumstances change.
- In many plans, your spouse cannot choose a lump sum or pass benefits to your children. If you both die, the money stops.

That's not protection. That's surrender.

## Why The Pension Shield Option™ Exists

This book isn't about tearing down pensions. It's about making smarter choices within the system you've earned.

The Pension Shield Option™ is designed to:

• Give you the maximum pension income available to you;

• Replace the risky survivor option with a flexible, tax-free benefit for your spouse; and

• Preserve your ability to pass wealth to your heirs, not back to the pension fund.

Your pension should be a shield — not a gamble. In the chapters ahead, we'll show you how to build it.

## Chapter 2 – How Public Safety Pensions Work

If you're a public safety professional — police, fire, EMS — your pension isn't just a benefit, it's the foundation of your retirement. Unlike private-sector employees who often patch together a 401(k), IRAs, and Social Security, your pension is usually the primary guaranteed income stream. That's why understanding how it works is non-negotiable. This chapter strips away the jargon so you can follow the numbers and ask the right questions before you sign anything.

### Defined Benefit vs. Defined Contribution

• Defined Benefit (DB): Your benefit is based on a formula — usually years of service × final average salary × a multiplier (often 2–3%). The employer shoulders the investment risk, and you receive a guaranteed monthly check for life.

• Defined Contribution (DC): Think 401(k), 403(b), or 457. Your benefit depends on how much you (and possibly your employer) contribute, plus investment performance. You shoulder the risk, and there are no guarantees.

### How the Formula Works

Example: 30 years of service × $80,000 final average salary × 2.5% multiplier = $60,000 per year ($5,000 per month). That's your "maximum" benefit. From here, you'll be asked to decide if you want to reduce it to provide a survivor option for your spouse.

COLA: The Silent Factor

Some pensions include a Cost of Living Adjustment (COLA), typically 2–3% annually. Others don't. If your pension has COLA, the amount you elect today grows every year. But here's the catch: if you choose a reduced survivor option, your COLA applies to the smaller benefit. Over 20–30 years, that difference compounds dramatically.

***"A smaller check today means an even smaller COLA tomorrow."***

### The DROP and Lump-Sum Trap

Many departments offer Deferred Retirement Option Plans (DROP). You "retire" on paper, freeze your pension calculation, and keep working while your pension accrues in a side account. When you officially retire, you receive the lump sum plus your ongoing monthly pension. Sounds great — until you realize DROP payouts, if not rolled over to another retirement account, can spike your taxable income in the year you retire. Combined with sick/vacation buybacks, you can trigger higher tax brackets, Medicare surcharges (IRMAA), and stealth taxes on Social Security. If you do roll it over into an IRA, you lose penalty-free access until age 59 ½.

***"It's better to be approximately right than precisely wrong."***

*-Uncle Joe*

## Know Your Numbers

Before you retire, ask your pension board or HR department:

1) What formula is used to calculate my pension?
2) What is my estimated maximum monthly benefit?
3) What are the reduction percentages for 50% survivor, 100% survivor, or other options?
4) Does my plan include COLA, and how is it applied?
5) Are survivor benefits tied to medical insurance eligibility?
6) Does my plan include a "pop-up" clause if my spouse dies first?

*Why This Chapter Matters:* If Chapter 1 showed you why the decision matters, this chapter shows you what you're actually deciding on. You now know the mechanics: the formulas, the COLA factor, and the traps like DROP payouts. In the next chapter, we'll expose the survivor option dilemma — why the "safe" choice isn't always the smart choice.

## Chapter 3 – The Survivor Dilemma

When you sit down with your pension packet, the "survivor option" looks like the obvious choice. After all, if something happens to you, you want your spouse to be protected. But here's the catch: protection comes at a steep price. Almost every pension system gives you two main choices:

1) Single Life (Maximum Pension): You receive the largest possible monthly check for your life only. Payments stop when you die.

2) Joint & Survivor Option: You take a reduced monthly check now, so your spouse continues to receive income if you die first.

On paper, the survivor option seems safer. In reality, it may be the most expensive "insurance" you ever buy — and the least flexible. Here are the six disadvantages you need to weigh carefully:

1. Reduced Benefit for Life

When you choose a survivor option, you permanently reduce your monthly income — often by 10–25%. Even if your spouse dies first, the reduction stays. No refunds, no reset.

2. Limited Flexibility

Once you elect the survivor option, it's usually irrevocable. Circumstances change — but your pension doesn't. If your spouse passes away, you're stuck with a smaller check for the rest of your life.

3. No Cash Value (No Equity)

A reduced survivor option is like paying premiums into a black hole. Unlike a Pension Shield Option™ coverage policy, there's no cash value, no ability to borrow, and no emergency access. It's pure cost with no asset behind it.

4. Disinheriting Your Children

The survivor option only protects your spouse. If both you and your spouse die, your children or estate receive nothing. You've paid for decades of reduced income, and the pension fund simply keeps the difference.

5. Reduced COLA

Many pensions include a Cost of Living Adjustment (COLA). Here's the kicker: the COLA is applied to the reduced benefit. Over 20–30 years, that difference compounds into a massive gap.

6. One Settlement Option Only

If your spouse outlives you, he or she usually gets one choice: a taxable monthly income for life. That's it. No lump sum, no flexibility, no ability to adjust for medical expenses or legacy planning.

*"You could lose hundreds of thousands of dollars over your lifetime — and get nothing back."*

### The Survivor Option in Numbers

Imagine: maximum pension $5,000/month versus 100% survivor option at $4,000/month. Over 20 years, that $1,000 monthly reduction equals $240,000 in lost income — and if both spouses die, heirs still receive nothing. Contrast that with the Pension Shield Option™, where the same dollars can build a tax-free benefit that pivots to your spouse or your estate.

Why People Still Choose It

- Convenience: It's the path of least resistance — just check a box.
- No health requirements: Everyone qualifies, regardless of insurability.
- Fear: Without guidance, many assume it's the only safe choice.

***Why This Chapter Matters:*** This is the moment where you realize that the traditional survivor option isn't the safe bet it appears to be. It's a rigid, irreversible choice with permanent consequences. In the next chapter, you'll see the alternative — the Pension Shield Option™ — and how it solves each of these problems while giving you both protection and flexibility.

## The Pension Shield Option™ – Part II

Chapters 4–7

## Chapter 4 – Pension Optimization 101

By now, you've seen the cracks in the traditional survivor option: reduced income, no equity, no flexibility. This chapter introduces the alternative — pension optimization — reframed here as the Pension Shield Option™. It's a strategy that's been around for decades, but it's been underutilized and underexplained to the very people who need it most: public safety retirees.

### The Core Idea

Pension optimization is simple at its core:
1) Take the maximum pension benefit available to you.
2) Use a portion of that increased income to purchase Pension Shield Option™ coverage.
3) Design the coverage to replace or exceed the survivor benefit you gave up.

With the Shield, you enjoy your full pension while you're alive, and your spouse is protected if you die first. Unlike the survivor option, your heirs aren't disinherited, your COLA applies to the bigger check, and your plan has flexibility.

### From Maximization to Protection

At Retirement Nationwide, Jim Lusk has taught this strategy for decades under the name Private Protection Plan (PPP). We're refining it here for public safety as the Pension Shield Option™ because your pension should function as a shield — protecting your spouse, your income, and your legacy.

***"Don't pay thousands to rent protection you'll never own. Build a shield you control."***

***-Jim Lusk***

### How It Solves the Six Problems

1) Reduced benefit for life → Keep the maximum pension.
2) Limited flexibility → If your spouse dies first, you can repurpose or surrender the policy.
3) No equity → Permanent policies build cash value.
4) Disinheritance → Pension Shield Option™ coverage enables tax-free inheritance to heirs.
5) Reduced COLA → COLA applies to the larger maximum benefit.
6) One settlement option → Multiple payout choices (lump sum, annuity, interest-only, period-certain).

### The Shield vs. The Survivor Option (at a glance)

Survivor Option: Reduced income, smaller COLA, no equity, disinherited heirs, one settlement choice.
Pension Shield: Maximum income, full COLA, potential cash value, heirs can inherit, multiple settlement choices.

### The Public Safety Edge

For police, fire, and EMS personnel, the Shield isn't a luxury — it's often essential: many do not have Social Security; COLA power is amplified on the maximum benefit; and some plans tie spouse medical coverage to a minimum survivor election — which can be paired with the Shield to keep benefits while restoring flexibility.

### A Real-World Example -Detective Hugh Dunnitt

Max pension = $5,000/month. 100% survivor option = $4,000/month. The $1,000 reduction is $12,000/year. Over 25 years, that's about $300,000 lost income before COLA. With the Shield, he might allocate $800/month to a policy that delivers roughly $800,000 tax-free to his spouse or heirs — while his net income still exceeds the survivor option.

### Why Haven't You Heard This Before?

Pension administrators administer pensions; they don't design private solutions. Many advisors avoid the topic because it requires deep knowledge of both pensions and insurance. The Shield demands an advisor who understands both worlds.

### *Important Caution*

Never elect the maximum pension until your Pension Shield Option™ coverage policy is fully underwritten, approved, and in force. If you take the maximum pension without coverage in place and later find you're un-insurable (or premiums are unaffordable), your spouse may be left unprotected.

***Why This Chapter Matters:*** This is the pivot from problem to solution. The Shield isn't complicated — *it's common sense wrapped in careful planning*. In the next chapter, we'll get into the mechanics: step-by-step, numbers and options.

## Chapter 5 – How the Shield Works

In Chapter 4, we introduced the Pension Shield Option™. Now we'll walk through how it actually works in practice — the numbers, the sequence, and the safeguards.

### *Step 1: Take the Maximum Pension*

At retirement, you'll see options such as Maximum (Single Life), Joint & 100% Survivor, and Joint & 50% Survivor. The Shield starts by selecting the Maximum option to lock in the biggest check and the largest possible COLA base.

### *Step 2: Redirect a Portion to Private Protection*

Instead of forfeiting $1,000/month to the pension system via a survivor election, reallocate part of that difference to fund Pension Shield Option™ coverage designed to protect your spouse with a tax-free benefit.

### *Step 3: Keep Your Flexibility*

If your spouse outlives you, they receive the tax-free benefit. If your spouse dies first, you keep the full pension and can reduce or repurpose coverage. If both of you pass away, heirs inherit the death benefit instead of the pension system keeping the balance.

### Side-by-Side Comparison (example)

Max pension: $5,000/month vs. 100% survivor at $4,000/month. The $1,000 difference is $12,000/year; over 25 years ≈ $300,000. Shield design: keep $5,000; allocate

~$800/month to insurance; provide ~$800,000 tax-free to spouse or heirs; net income remains higher than the survivor option.

### The Shield Advantage in Action

• Both live long → Full COLA on maximum income; protection remains available.

• Retiree dies first → Spouse chooses lump sum or income from a tax-free benefit.
• Spouse dies first → Retiree keeps maximum pension and adjusts coverage as desired.
• Both die early → Heirs inherit a tax-free benefit.

### *Step 4: Spouse Settlement Options*

Your spouse isn't locked into one taxable monthly check. With the Shield, they can choose a lump sum, a lifetime annuity (that could be partly tax free from the *exclusion ratio),* a refund annuity, period-certain payments, or interest-only income.

### *Step 5: Legacy Protection*

The survivor option ends with your spouse. The Shield can continue to your heirs, turning lost reductions into a family legacy.

**Final Warning Before Moving On**

Your pension election is irrevocable. Get pre-approved, fully underwritten, and the policy in force before you sign. Insurance first; pension election second.

**Why This Chapter Matters:** This chapter moves the Shield from concept to concrete. You've seen the mechanics and the sequence that keeps your spouse protected and your income intact.

## Chapter 6 – Four Real-Life Scenarios

Retirement rarely follows averages. Some retirees pass early, some spouses predecease, and some couples outlive everyone's projections. Here's how the two choices — survivor election vs. Pension Shield — hold up across the only four outcomes that exist.

### *Scenario 1: Both Live Long Lives*

Survivor Option: Reduced income and smaller COLA for decades.

Pension Shield: Maximum income and full COLA while alive; protection remains if needed. Equity grows tax deferred with tax-free access.

### *Scenario 2: Spouse Dies First*

Survivor Option: Retiree remains stuck with a reduced check forever.

Pension Shield: Retiree keeps the full pension and can reduce or surrender coverage.

### *Scenario 3: Both Die Early*

Survivor Option: Payments stop; heirs inherit nothing.

Pension Shield: Heirs inherit the tax-free death benefit.

### *Scenario 4: Retiree Dies First*

Survivor Option: Spouse receives a reduced taxable monthly check with no flexibility.

Pension Shield: Spouse receives a tax-free benefit designed to meet or exceed needs, with freedom to choose lump sum, lifetime income, or a blend.

### Four Ways to Lose, One Way to Win

Both die early → Shield preserves a legacy.
Both live long → Shield preserves income and COLA and grows equity.
Retiree dies first → Shield offers higher, flexible protection.
Spouse dies first → Shield avoids a permanent pay cut.

Critical Reminder

The plan only works if the Pension Shield Option ™ is secured before your pension election. Once you sign, there are no do-overs. (Although some states give you 60 to 90 days to change options.)

**Why This Chapter Matters:** This is the proof chapter: the Shield provides better outcomes across all four scenarios, while the survivor option only "wins" in one.

## Chapter 7 – When the Shield Fits — And When It Doesn't

The Pension Shield is powerful, but not universal. This chapter shows where it shines and where the traditional survivor option may still be the safer choice.

### When the Shield Fits

• You are in good health (better underwriting, lower premiums).

• Your pension includes a COLA (amplifies inflation protection on the maximum benefit).

• You value flexibility and control (multiple settlement choices; no permanent pay cut if your spouse dies first).

• You care about legacy (benefits can pass to heirs tax-free).

• You want maximum net income (often higher spendable income even after premiums).

• DROP is an option and you can fund your protection at an earlier (lower cost/ better health) age and by diverting the money that used to go to pension contributions.

### When the Shield May *Not* Fit

• Poor health or uninsurable: the survivor option may be the only viable protection.

• Medical coverage rules: some plans require a minimum survivor election to preserve spouse health insurance — pair that minimum election with the Shield if possible.

• Severe budget constraints: if premiums strain cash flow, a survivor option may be the fallback. But it could be much more costly in the long run.

• Late retirement age: higher premiums can reduce efficiency; consider hybrids (smaller survivor election + targeted private coverage).

## Two Sides of the Actuarial Coin: Mathematics vs. Demographics — Two Ways to Measure a Lifetime

When it comes to predicting how long people live, both pensions and life insurance companies rely on statistics. But they look at those statistics from completely different directions — and that difference changes everything about how your benefits are calculated.

### *Let's start with life insurance.*

Life insurance companies begin with huge data sets that show how long people usually live — that's demographics. But they don't stop there. When you apply for coverage, they use something called *underwriting* to adjust those averages to fit you. They look at your age, health, lifestyle, and even your habits. They might consider your blood pressure, weight, medical history, family longevity, smoking, exercise, or occupation and hobbies. Then they calculate how your personal risk compares to the "average person" your age. That process turns general statistics into personal mathematics. The result is a custom estimate of your likelihood of dying in any given year. If you're healthy, the math says your odds of dying soon are low — so your premiums are lower. If you're in poor health, your odds are higher — and so are your costs.

*In short, life insurance companies start with demographic data but then make it personal. Their math adapts to you.*

*Now look at pensions.*

Pension systems work in reverse. They use life expectancy tables built from national averages, but they don't make personal adjustments. They lump everyone together — the fit, the frail, the marathoners, and the midnight snackers. Everyone your age is treated as if they're the same person.

Why? Because the pension fund isn't focused on you — it's focused on keeping the system balanced for the whole group. It has to make sure that, across thousands of retirees, the money coming in and the money going out stay roughly in sync. The math is about averages, not individuals.

That means if you're healthier than average, the pension's math quietly works against you. You'll probably live longer than the system expects — and that's not reflected in your payout. The system assumes "average," so your longevity becomes its extra liability. In a sense, you're subsidizing those who don't live as long.

So we can say:

- Life insurance starts with demographics but ends in personal mathematics — it begins with the crowd and adapts to you.
- Pensions start with mathematics but end in demographics — they begin with formulas and flatten everyone into the same average.

Life insurance rewards individuality. Pensions depend on conformity.

If you're healthy, that difference matters. The life insurance company will recognize your good health and reward it with lower costs. The pension fund won't notice — it will still treat you like the middle of the pack.

That's where the Pension Shield Option™ shines. It bridges these two worlds — the mathematical and the demographic — to create something personal, flexible, and fair. It lets you benefit from your own health and habits instead of being trapped by the system's averages.

The Pension Shield Option™ lives right in that space — between math and humanity — where the numbers finally fit the person they represent.

Uncle Joe's Gem:

***"If you let the system treat you like everyone else, don't be surprised when you get everyone else's result."***

## The Rules of Risk Management

Years ago in *Prosperity By Design*, I framed three rules that still guide this decision:
1) Never risk more than you can afford to lose.
2) Consider the odds.
3) Don't risk a lot to save a little or spend a lot to protect a little.

These rules have stood the test of time across investing, insurance, and retirement planning — and they apply here as much as anywhere.

**Why This Chapter Matters:** This balanced view builds credibility. The Shield isn't a one-size-fits-all gimmick; it's a disciplined strategy that belongs where the facts support it. In the next section, we move from design to selection — choosing the right protection plan (term, permanent, or convertible term) to build your Shield.

# The Pension Shield Option™ – Part III

Chapters 8–11

## Chapter 8 – Choosing the Right Protection Plan

By now, you understand what the Pension Shield Option™ does — it preserves your pension, protects your spouse, and keeps a legacy for your heirs. But like any good shield, its strength depends on the materials it's built from. This chapter explores the types of insurance that fund your Shield, their strengths and weaknesses, and how to choose the right plan for your family.

### The Two Main Choices: Term vs. Permanent

1) Term Pension Shield Option™ coverage — Pure protection for a set period (10, 20, or 30 years). No cash value, but lower premiums. Useful if you need maximum protection for the lowest cost.

2) Permanent Pension Shield Option™ coverage (Whole Life, Universal Life, Indexed UL, etc.) — Coverage that lasts for life and can build cash value. Premiums are higher, but the Shield stays in place no matter when you die.

### The Lease Option: Freezing Your Health

Jim has taught for years a clever approach he calls the "Lease Option." Buy a convertible term policy at retirement. This "leases" your health rating — locking in your insurability now, while you're healthy — and gives you the right to convert to permanent coverage later without additional medical underwriting. It's ideal for public safety employees who retire young and in good health but want to keep options open as medical needs change.

### Matching the Plan to the Person

• If your spouse only needs coverage for a limited time (until Social Security starts or the mortgage is paid), term insurance may be enough.
• If you want permanent flexibility, equity, and a legacy for heirs, permanent insurance fits best.
• If you're not sure, start with convertible term (the Lease Option) so you can change course later.

### What to Look For in a Policy

• Strong insurer with high financial-strength ratings.
• Convertible options (for term) — must allow conversion to permanent without new medical exams.
• Flexible settlements — allow heirs to choose lump sum, income, or blended payouts.

### Weak Shields Break

Avoid cheap non-convertible term that leaves you stranded later, underfunded permanent policies that collapse, and "too good to be true" products pitched without regard to your pension rules. A weak policy makes for a weak Shield.

### The Prosperity & Precision Balance

In *Prosperity By Design,* George explained that good planning balances safety, income, and growth. Insurance choices are no different: Safety (a guaranteed death benefit), Income (preserving maximum pension while alive), and Growth (cash value and legacy potential). As Jim wrote in *Money Machines for Life*, your pension and insurance are two gears in the same machine. Choose strong parts, and the machine runs smoothly.

**Why This Chapter Matters:** The Shield is only as strong as the protection behind it. Choosing the right policy ensures your spouse is protected, your income is preserved, and your heirs are remembered. The wrong policy — or no policy at all — could turn a smart strategy into a dangerous gamble. In the next chapter, we'll show how the Shield fits into your overall retirement strategy.

## Chapter 9 – Integration With Retirement Strategy

Your pension election is one of the biggest financial decisions you'll ever make — but it doesn't stand alone. The Pension Shield Option™ works best when it's integrated into your overall retirement plan: your DROP, your IRAs, your Roth conversions, your taxes, and your legacy goals. This chapter shows how the Shield fits into the larger system so every gear turns smoothly.

### Real Life Case Dee Fibralate

**Dee Fibralate**

Paramedic Dee Fibralate began a 5-year DROP. During her DROP period, Dee no longer contributes 6½% of her salary to her pension. That's new monthly cash flow she can re-purpose — and instead of parking it in her 457 account like so many do without thinking, she uses it to fund a life insurance policy. She's five years younger than when she'll retire and probably healthier so she'll get better life insurance premiums.

She asks her insurance professional to illustrate a "Guaranteed Five Pay" -which means she only pays in during the five years she's in DROP.

By the time Dee officially retires:

Her pension benefit remains unreduced by the survivor option.

Her spouse is protected by a tax-free life insurance benefit that possibly exceeds the 50% Joint & Survivor option.

If her spouse passes away first, the policy can be redirected or surrendered — something the pension plan wouldn't allow.

### The Three Buckets: Tax Now, Tax Later, Tax Never

In *Prosperity By Design,* George introduced the Three Buckets framework: ***Tax Now*** (brokerage/savings), ***Tax Later*** (457, 403(b), traditional IRAs, DROP balances), and ***Tax Never*** (Roth IRAs/conversions, HSAs, and properly structured Pension Shield Option™ coverage). Your pension is taxable income (Tax Now), while Shield benefits are generally Tax Never — a unique tool for balancing the buckets.

### The DROP Dilemma

DROP balances often arrive as a large lump sum that could spike taxable income if not rolled over to an IRA, especially when combined with vacation/sick time buyouts. That can push you into higher brackets, trigger Medicare IRMAA surcharges, and phase out deductions. The Shield doesn't eliminate taxes, but it gives flexibility: by preserving maximum pension income and shifting survivor protection to Pension Shield Option™ coverage, you can redirect DROP funds into strategic moves like

Roth conversions instead of being handcuffed by reduced benefits.

### Stealth Taxes and the Shield

In *Stop, DROP and Roll*, George explained how stealth taxes (IRMAA, Social Security taxation, phaseouts) raise tax payments without raising marginal brackets. The Shield helps blunt those traps: survivor benefits are received income tax–free, so they don't inflate taxable income or MAGI; keeping maximum pension income lets you plan conversions on your schedule; and Shield death benefits don't count toward IRMAA thresholds. If the survivor elects a guaranteed payout option the distributions would only be partially taxable because of the *exclusion ratio.*

The exclusion ratio is the IRS formula that splits each annuity payment into two parts: the tax-free return of your original benefit and the taxable earnings. It determines what portion of each check you actually owe tax on.

### Coordinating With Other Retirement Accounts

• IRAs and 457s — Shield benefits can offset taxable withdrawals, letting you manage distributions strategically.

• Roth accounts — Pairing Roth conversions with the Shield creates a "double tax-free" system: Roth income while alive, Shield benefits at death.

• Estate planning — Shield proceeds can fund trusts, charitable gifts, equalize inheritances, or cover state inheritance taxes without liquidating other assets.

### Shield + Roth = Retirement Freedom

Imagine retiring with $1,000,000 in a 457 plan. You run strategic Roth conversions in low-tax years, while your spouse is protected by the Shield. Result: tax-managed retirement income for you and two streams of tax-free legacy for heirs — Roth assets and the Shield benefit.

**Critical Reminder**

The Shield is most effective when coordinated with your overall plan. Work with an advisor who understands pensions, insurance, and taxes. Your pension election is permanent — your strategy should remain flexible.

### Jim's Precision Perspective

As Jim wrote in *Money Machines for Life*, every retirement system is a collection of gears. Your pension is one gear, your DROP another, your IRAs another, and the Shield is the protective casing that keeps the machine running. If one gear slips, the whole machine falters. Integrated correctly, they hum together for decades.

**Why This Chapter Matters:** The Shield isn't a standalone tactic — it's part of a holistic strategy. Integrated properly, it preserves income, minimizes taxes, and maximizes legacy. Next, we'll show how the Shield shines brightly in estate and legacy planning.

## Chapter 10 – The Blind Spot: Long-Term Care and the Pension Shield Option™

You know the drill: when you punch the clock, you plan for three things—going home at the end of shift, getting hurt, or not making it home at all. Retirement isn't much different. Once you hang up the gear, there are three possibilities:

1. You live a long, healthy life.
2. You die too soon.
3. You get sick or disabled somewhere in between.

Your pension? It's built for the first possibility only. It pays as long as you're breathing. If you pass away, the survivor option may cover your spouse. But if you get sick or disabled, if you need long-term care, the pension doesn't change—it just keeps sending the same check while your costs skyrocket. That's the blind spot.

### The Pension Shield Option™ as the Missing Gear in Your Loadout

The Pension Shield Option™ isn't just about protecting your spouse if you die first. With the right structure, it can:

- Cover long-term care expenses if you can't perform basic daily tasks.
- Provide a benefit payout if you never need care, turning income into legacy.

- Preserve your pension income for your spouse by handling medical costs separately.

### Case File: The Fire Fighter Who Planned for Care

Bernie Ashford, a retired fire fighter, set up the Pension Shield Option™ before leaving the job. Ten years later, a stroke left him needing rehab and partial in-home care. His pension kept the household afloat. The Shield covered the $6,000/month in care expenses as an advance against the death benefit. Without it, Bernie's wife would have burned through savings in under three years.

### Tactical Breakdown: The Three Scenarios

#### - Scenario 1: Long Life

Pension does its job. Income keeps flowing. The Pension Shield Option™ adds a legacy benefit for spouse and family.

#### - Scenario 2: Short Life

Pension stops. Survivor option may pay spouse—but at the cost of decades of reduced income. The Pension Shield Option™ delivers a lump sum that replaces or supplements survivor benefits.

#### - Scenario 3: Sick/Disabled In-Between

This is where pensions fail. LTC needs can easily run $5,000–$10,000 a month. Without coverage, that money comes from your pension and savings. With the Shield, those costs are handled while pension income keeps paying the bills.

### Decision Matrix: Do You Need the Pension Shield Option™ for Long-Term Care?

| Question | If YES | If NO |
|---|---|---|
| Do you have a pension that stops at death? | Consider the Pension Shield Option™ with long-term-care features to protect your spouse. | You may be able to rely on other assets for survivor support. |
| Do you want to leave a legacy to kids or grandkids? | The Pension Shield Option™ can preserve wealth while still covering care needs. | A traditional LTC-only approach may suffice. |
| Do you have family history of chronic illness? | Prioritize a Shield strategy that includes LTC coverage. | Lower urgency, but the Shield still adds flexibility. |
| Would you rather pay for care yourself or transfer the risk? | If you'd rather transfer risk, the Pension Shield Option™ is efficient. | If you're fully self-insured, you may choose to skip it. |

### Checklist: Plugging the Blind Spot

☑ Evaluate your pension for long-term care gaps (hint: they all have them).

☑ Review how the Pension Shield Option™ can integrate riders for care needs.

☑ Compare costs of Shield vs. potential LTC expenses in your state.

☑ Decide if preserving pension income is priority #1.

☑ Coordinate Shield with your overall retirement plan.

In uniform, you never left the station half-prepared. In retirement, don't carry only one tool when you know there are three ways the story can play out. Your pension covers the first. The Pension Shield Option™ covers the second and third. Only with all three are you fully geared up.

> *"Your pension covers the first. The Pension Shield Option™ covers the second and third. Only with all three are you fully geared up."*
>
> *"In the field, you don't risk a lot to save a little. The lump sum can be the right move for some — but it's also a gamble."*

## Chapter 12 – Lump Sum Options: Control vs. Lifetime Income

You've faced plenty of crossroads in your career: go through the door or wait for backup, push the gas or hold the line. Retirement throws another one at you — the lump sum option.

Some pension systems let you take the present value of your benefit in one big payout. Others allow you to withdraw your contributions as a lump sum in exchange for reduced monthly income. On the surface, it feels like control: more flexibility, more options, more money in your pocket.

But here's the tactical truth: a lump sum is a one-shot deal. Once you take it, you can't go back. And the size of that payout isn't fixed — it rises and falls with interest rates. A chief who retired when rates were low might walk away with hundreds of thousands more than the one who retires in a high-rate year.

It's a decision that can make or break your retirement mission.

### Tactical Breakdown: Lump Sum vs. Lifetime Income

- Lifetime Annuity (the standard pension check):
  Pros: Predictable, steady income for life, immune to market crashes.
  Cons: Inflexible. Survivor option reduces your pay for life.

- Lump Sum:
  Pros: More control, potential to invest, leave money to heirs.
  Cons: Market risk, interest-rate sensitivity, possibility of outliving your money.

This isn't about which option looks bigger on paper — it's about whether you want guaranteed ammo drops for life or prefer to carry the whole supply kit on your back and manage it yourself.

### How Do You Know Which Is Right?

The only way to know if a lump sum is a smart move is to run the math. That means calculating the ROI (return on investment) — comparing what the annuity would pay over your expected lifetime against what you could reasonably earn by investing the lump sum.

Yes, it's mathematics, and yes, there's a little algebra. But a good financial advisor with experience in public safety retirements can crunch those numbers, stress-test the assumptions, and help you see whether the lump sum would actually beat the guaranteed pension.

If you have severe health challenges the lump sum may be a way to ensure your benefit passes to your spouse, but you'll need to protect it by trust or gifting to your spouse. In almost all states pension benefits are protected from creditors.

### ROI (Return On Investment) Snapshot

Pension offers two options at retirement:

- Lifetime Annuity: $4,000 per month for life.
- Lump Sum: $800,000 rollover into your IRA.

If you take the annuity and live 25 years, you'll collect: $4,000 × 12 months × 25 years = $1.2 million (guaranteed). If you take the lump sum, to match that $1.2 million over the same 25 years, your $800,000 would need to average about 4.5% annual return after fees and taxes.

That's doable — but not guaranteed. And if you live longer than 25 years? The annuity keeps paying. The lump sum doesn't necessarily.

This is why ROI math isn't optional. It's the only way to know if a lump sum deal actually stacks up to lifetime pay.

### Case File: The Chief Who Rolled the Dice

Chase Downes, a retired investigator, took the lump sum in 2020 and rolled it into an IRA. At the time, rates were low and his payout looked huge. Two years later, markets dropped 30% and inflation spiked. Chases pension paycheck would have been steady, but now his income depends on a volatile portfolio. Chase has more control — but he's also carrying more risk than he ever expected. Chase's investments can go down but not the pension.

**Decision Matrix: Lump Sum vs. Lifetime Income**

| Factor | Lump Sum Advantage | Lifetime Income Advantage |
|---|---|---|
| Desire for control | Manage and invest funds yourself | Pension system manages payments |
| Market risk | Potential for higher growth | No exposure to downturns |
| Interest rates | Low rates = higher payout | Irrelevant to monthly checks |
| Longevity | Short life favors lump sum (more legacy potential) | Long life favors annuity (guaranteed lifetime pay) |
| Spouse coverage | Flexible with Pension Shield Option™ add-on | Survivor option covers spouse, but reduces your pay |

**Checklist: Lump Sum Planning Steps**

☑ Request written estimates for both lump sum and annuity options.

☑ Compare the lump sum to the annuity's guaranteed monthly pay using today's rates.

☑ Stress-test: What happens if markets drop 20% the year after you retire?

☑ Factor in spouse needs: Survivor income vs. Pension Shield Option™ benefits.

☑ Review tax consequences before rolling into an IRA.

☑ Calculate ROI with an advisor who knows public safety pensions.

☑ Decide: Do you want the steady check or the burden of managing the full payout?

In the field, you don't risk a lot to save a little. The lump sum can be the right move for some — but it's also a gamble. If you take it, you need a solid strategy, like the Pension Shield Option™, to protect your family's six when markets or health take unexpected turns.

*"Taking a risk means you have a way out if things go south. A gamble? That's when failure means there is no second chance."*

-Uncle Joe

## Chapter 13 – Estate and Legacy Benefits

A pension is designed to take care of you while you live, and sometimes to take care of your spouse after you die. What it's not designed to do is pass wealth on to your children, grandchildren, or causes that matter to you. That's why so many retirees are shocked to learn the truth: once you and your spouse are gone, your pension ends. It doesn't matter how many decades you served or how much you gave up in reduced benefits — the money stops, and the pension fund keeps the balance.

The Pension Shield Option™ changes that. By using private protection instead of relying solely on the survivor option, you safeguard your spouse and create a legacy for the people and purposes you care about.

### The Legacy Gap in Survivor Options

Traditional survivor elections create what Jim Lusk calls the "inheritance blackout." You will disinherit your children or estate. Spouse dies first → reduction continues with no refund; both spouses die → heirs get nothing; pension balance → reverts to the system. In *Die Neatly*, Jim described how poor planning can rob families of dignity and order at the very moment they need it most.

### How the Shield Preserves Legacy

• If you die first, your spouse receives a tax-free benefit with flexibility to use it as income, a lump sum, or a combination of both.

• If your spouse dies first, you keep your full pension and may reduce or redirect coverage and you have equity in the plan.

• If you both pass early, your heirs inherit the death benefit — tax-free — creating a legacy the pension would never provide.

***"Pass it to YOUR estate, not THE state."***

***-Jim Lusk***

### Settlement Options That Empower Families

Unlike the survivor option's one-size-fits-all monthly check, the Shield gives your family choices: lump sum, lifetime annuity, refund annuity, period-certain payments, or interest-only settlement. This flexibility lets your family make the best decision for their circumstances at the time — not lock into a single rigid choice decades earlier.

### Integrating Legacy With Estate Planning

• Trust funding — direct Shield benefits into a trust for children, grandchildren, or special-needs dependents.

• Charitable giving — fund a lasting gift to a cause close to your heart.

• Equalization — if one child inherits a house or business, Shield proceeds can equalize the inheritance

• Estate taxes — while most families won't hit federal

thresholds, state inheritance taxes matter; Shield benefits can cover those costs without touching other assets.

### The Legacy Test

Ask yourself:

1) If my spouse and I pass away, what do my children inherit from my pension?

2) If the answer is "nothing," am I comfortable with that?

3) If not, what steps can I take today to change that outcome?

The Shield answers that test with dignity, flexibility, and fairness.

### Critical Reminder

Your pension election is permanent. Once you give away a portion of your check to the survivor option, there is no way to reclaim that value for your heirs. With the Shield, you keep control.

**Why This Chapter Matters:** Pensions stop. The Shield carries on. It protects your spouse and preserves a legacy that reflects your values

## Chapter 14 – Common Questions and Objections

Important decisions deserve scrutiny. This chapter addresses the most common questions and objections retirees raise about the Pension Shield Option™ — directly and without sugarcoating.

*Q1: What if my spouse dies before me?*

Survivor Option: you're stuck with a reduced check for life. System keeps the difference. (Unless the system offers a "Pop up" provision and then the system keeps the equity.

Pension Shield: you keep your maximum pension. You can keep the policy, reduce coverage, or cancel it and redirect funds elsewhere.

*Q2: What if I can't qualify for insurance?*

If you're uninsurable due to health, the Shield may not be viable. In that case, the survivor option is your fallback — it may be expensive, but at least it's guaranteed.

*Q3: What if I live a long time and premiums eat up too much income?*

The Shield is designed so premiums come from the difference between the maximum pension and the reduced survivor option. Even after premiums, most retirees enjoy more net income than if they had taken the survivor option. Permanent policies can also build cash value.

*Q4: What if my pension board doesn't like this idea?*

Pension boards administer pensions; they don't design private solutions. As Jim wrote in *Money Machines for Life,* "Don't expect the machine to tell you how to re-engineer it." The Shield is an outside solution – you must take responsibility for your own planning.

*Q5: Is the insurance really tax-free?*

That rule lives in **Internal Revenue Code Section 101(a)(1)**. It says that amounts received under a life insurance contract, paid by reason of the insured's death, are excluded from gross income—meaning death benefits are generally income tax–free to the beneficiary. Of course, there are exceptions (for example, if the policy was transferred for value, or if the payout is held and earns interest), but the backbone rule is right there in §101.

So, in most cases, yes. Pension Shield Option™ coverage death benefits are income tax-free to beneficiaries, which means Shield benefits don't inflate taxable income, don't trigger IRMAA, and don't reduce deductions. Always confirm with a qualified tax professional.

*Q6: What if premiums rise and I can't afford them later?*

With permanent insurance, premiums are typically fixed. With convertible term (Lease Option), you lock in insurability now and decide later whether to convert. The Shield is flexible, but budgeting and review are critical. And the longer you wait, the more expensive it will be.

*Q7: Why haven't I heard this before?*

Administrators focus on their forms; many advisors avoid this because it demands expertise in both pensions and insurance. In *Stop, DROP and Roll,* George warned that first responders face "stealth risks" no one talks about — this is one of them.

*Q8: What if I want both — survivor option and the Shield?*

In some cases, combine a minimum survivor election (to preserve spouse health coverage) with the Shield to cover the rest. Hybrid strategies work — with careful planning. But dual coverage costs a lot more.

### Top 5 Myths About the Shield Busted

1) "It's too risky." — It's built on the same foundation as traditional survivor protection—but with added flexibility, ownership, and control. Life insurance companies have stood the test of time over 140 years, thriving through world wars and the Great Depression. Their stability and long record of paying claims make them among the most time-tested financial institutions in the world
2) "It's too expensive." — Premiums are paid with money you'd otherwise lose to a reduced pension. Done correctly, it's self-sustaining.
3) "It's unproven." — Advisors like Jim have implemented it for decades nationwide.

4) "It's complicated." — The math is straightforward: maximum pension minus premium = higher net income + protection.
5) 5) "It's only for the wealthy." — It's used by public safety employees across the country.

**Why This Chapter Matters:** By answering the real questions asked at the kitchen table, the Shield becomes practical and believable. Next up is your step-by-step checklist — and then action.

# The Pension Shield Option™ – Part IV

Chapters 13–14 + Conclusion

## Chapter 15 – The Pension Shield Checklist

You've seen how the Pension Shield Option™ works, why it often outperforms the traditional survivor election, and how it fits into your overall retirement strategy. Now it's time to turn theory into action. This chapter is your Shield Checklist — a step-by-step guide to make sure you're protected, your spouse is secure, and your legacy is preserved. Think of it as your pre-flight checklist before takeoff.

### Step 1: Gather the Essentials

• Pension estimate statement (showing maximum and survivor options).

• Spouse information (age, health, smoker/non-smoker status).

• Your own health summary (medications, conditions, history).

• COLA details (does your plan include one? How is it calculated?).

• Medical coverage rules (is survivor health insurance tied to your election?).

• DROP balance or projected payout (if applicable).

### Step 2: Request Key Information

Ask your pension board/HR:

1) What are the reduction percentages for survivor options?

2) Does my plan include a "pop-up" clause if my spouse dies first?

3) What forms are required to elect or decline survivor options?
4) Are survivor benefits required to preserve retiree medical coverage?
5) Can I receive a written projection of each option?

***Don't just accept the numbers you're given — ask for details, in writing.***

### Step 3: Run the Math

With your advisor, compare the lifetime cost of the survivor option versus the premium cost of insurance. Model four scenarios (both live long, you die first, spouse dies first, both die early), and stress-test using inflation and COLA assumptions.

### Step 4: Secure Insurance Coverage

Get the medical questions answered with preliminary underwriting. Do not finalize your pension election until your Pension Shield Option ™ is fully underwritten, approved at an acceptable rating, issued, and in force. Without a binding policy, the Shield does not exist.

### Step 5: Decide on Policy Type

• Term (convertible): Lower cost, locks in health rating now but needs to be converted later.
• Permanent: Higher cost, lifelong protection and potential cash value.
• Hybrid: Start with as much permanent coverage as you

can afford (the "Lease Option") and convert later as needed.

### Step 6: Review Your Budget

• Confirm premiums fit comfortably within the difference between maximum pension and survivor option.
• Stress-test: could you still pay premiums if inflation rises or expenses spike?
• Adjust hybrid to keep your plan sustainable.

### Step 7: Document Your Decision

• File your pension election with clear documentation.
• Store your insurance policy, pension paperwork, and contact info together.
• Make sure your spouse and heirs know who to contact and how the Shield works.

### The Shield Readiness Score

Have you gathered pension estimates and rules?
Do you know your spouse's and your health status?
Have you reviewed written projections?
Is your insurance policy in force?
Have you reviewed premium affordability?
Have you documented everything for your family?
If you can check every box, your Shield is ready.

### Step 8: Review Periodically

Your life will change. Review your Shield strategy every 2–3 years — or sooner if health, coverage, tax laws, or goals change. As Jim often says: "People don't plan to fail; they fail to plan."

**Why This Chapter Matters:** The Pension Shield isn't just an idea — it's an action plan. By following this checklist, you move from theory to execution. You've worked too hard to leave your pension — and your family's security — to chance.

## Chapter 16 – Next Steps and Call to Action

By now, you've seen the stakes, explored the options, and walked through the mechanics of the Pension Shield. You've seen how it compares to the survivor option, how it works under every scenario, and how it integrates into your broader retirement plan. Now it's time to act.

### Why Early Action Matters

Every day you wait, two things happen: you get older (premiums rise with age) and your health can change (a diagnosis can make you uninsurable or push premiums out of reach). The most successful Shield strategies start early.

### The Cost of Waiting

Two officers, both age 55, retiring in five years: Officer A applies now and locks in preferred rates; Officer B waits until 60 and develops high blood pressure. Result: A secures affordable permanent coverage; B is declined or pays double. Same pension; only one created a Shield.

### What to Do Right Now

1) Gather your pension estimates (maximum and survivor projections).
2) Review your health and your spouse's health realistically.
3) Meet with a qualified advisor who understands pensions, insurance, and taxes.
4) Run Shield illustrations and compare lifetime costs.

5) Apply early to lock in your health rating and save age.
6) Confirm policy in force — then finalize your pension election.

### The Cost of Doing Nothing

- Survivor option = reduced pension forever.
- Spouse dies first = you're stuck with the cut.
- Both die early = heirs inherit nothing.
- Pension ends = system keeps the balance.

***Doing nothing isn't neutral — it's costly.***

### The Call to Action

If you're reading this, you already know your pension choice is too important to leave to chance. The Shield gives you clarity, confidence, and control — but only if you act before your pension election becomes permanent. Take the next step. Run your numbers. Secure your Shield. Protect your spouse. Build your legacy.

**Why This Chapter Matters:** This chapter isn't about more theory. It's about action. The Pension Shield isn't something to think about "someday." It's a decision you must make before your pension paperwork is signed.

## Chapter 17 Call for Backup

In law enforcement, fire, and EMS, you never go in alone. Backup isn't optional — it's survival. The same rule applies to your pension.

### Overconfidence at the Pension Desk

Too many public safety employees believe they can "wing it" when it comes to retirement decisions. They trust a gut feeling, skim the paperwork, or rely on what a buddy at the station told them — or the locker room loudmouth told them. That's not a plan. That's a gamble.

Uncle Joe's Gem — Risk vs. Gamble

***"A risk is a chance you take, and if it fails, you can recover. A gamble is a chance taken where failure means you don't get a second chance."***

### The Sgt. Lou D. Mouth Story — Certified Locker Room Know-it-all

Let's talk about **Lou D. Mouth**— the kind of guy who shows up to your retirement dinner with unsolicited investment advice and a laminated spreadsheet of "guaranteed" real estate returns.

Lou's retirement strategy?

- Take his DROP lump sum
- Buy three rental properties
- Ignore the tax implications
- Avoid real planning like it's paperwork during shift change

Lou's financial education? Whatever he overheard between sets at the gym and three episodes of a "real estate fire" podcast. He's also a Reddit Regular. Lou doesn't *ask* questions—he *answers* them. Loudly. In the locker room. With confidence far exceeding his competence.

**"It's not what you don't know that gets you into trouble. It's what you know for sure that just ain't so."**

**— Uncle Joe**

### The Dunning–Kruger Effect

Psychologists call this **Dunning-Kruger Effect** — a real, phenomenon where the least skilled or least informed people are the most confident in their opinions. It's not arrogance so much as ignorance wearing certainty like body armor.

The less you truly know about a subject, the more likely you are to overestimate your grasp of it. The pension packet looks simple; the survivor option feels safe. But hidden costs, tax traps, and legacy losses hide in the fine print—and they stay hidden unless you bring backup. Without it, losses slip past unnoticed until it's too late.

### The Four Stages of Competence

Understanding the Dunning–Kruger ladder helps explain why well-meaning colleagues—or that cousin who just watched a YouTube video on Roth IRAs—sound so sure of bad advice.

1. **Unconscious Incompetence -** You don't know how little you know.
2. **Conscious Incompetence -** You begin to realize your limitations.
3. **Conscious Competence -** You learn and apply skills with effort.
4. **Unconscious Competence -**You're an expert — and don't have to think twice.

Most loudmouths in the breakroom are stuck on rung one but think they're standing on rung four. And that's dangerous — especially when your future is on the line.

### Signs You Need Backup

• You can't explain how your pension is calculated.
• You don't know how COLA applies to survivor options.
• You've never compared survivor costs vs. private protection.
• You don't know if spouse medical coverage depends on survivor election.
• You're unsure what (if anything) heirs inherit.

### Uncle Joe's Gem: Never Ask a Barber

"Never ask a barber if you need a haircut." Don't ask a pension office or your auto insurance agent for pension-protection advice and expect an unbiased answer. Work with a credentialed, ethical advisor with experience in public safety retirements — not just an insurance agent who handles home and auto.

### Why Backup Matters

The Shield isn't DIY. It requires knowledge of pension rules, insurance underwriting, and tax impacts (especially stealth taxes like IRMAA). You wouldn't let a rookie clear a building alone. Don't let a rookie mistake clear out your family's retirement security.

### Calling for Backup

Backup doesn't make you weak — it makes you wise. As written in *Stop, DROP and Roll,* the biggest disasters weren't caused by fire or bullets but by ignorance mixed with overconfidence. Calling for backup means working with someone who sees blind spots, stress-tests your plan, and protects your family from irreversible mistakes.

### Why You Need a Filter (and a Fiduciary)

Your career depended on trusting experience, training, and standard operating procedures. Retirement planning is no different. You need:

- **Facts, not folklore**
- **Math, not myths**
- **A plan, not a rant**

Listening to the wrong advice at the wrong time can cost you six figures or more — in taxes, lost benefits, or plain old bad decisions.

If your "retirement plan" came from the weight room or the shooting range, you don't have a plan — you have a problem.

**Why This Chapter Matters:** Confidence can be a strength — or a blindfold. When the decision is permanent and your family's future is on the line, you don't go in alone. Ask the right person. Choose an advisor who knows your world, has the credentials, and has the integrity to put your interests first.

## Conclusion

You've served your community with honor. Your pension is the reward for a lifetime of service. But it's more than a paycheck — it's a **Shield**, and how you wield it will define your retirement and your family's security for decades.

### What We've Learned Together

- How public safety pensions work — and where the traps lie.
- Why the survivor option is often the most expensive and least flexible choice.
- How the Pension Shield preserves maximum income while protecting your spouse and heirs.
- Why the Shield works across every real-world scenario.
- How to choose the right insurance and integrate the Shield into taxes, DROP, and estate planning.
- Why you must never go it alone — call for backup from an experienced, ethical advisor.

### What's at Stake

Your pension election is permanent. With the survivor option, you risk giving up hundreds of thousands in income, shrinking COLAs, and leaving nothing for your children. With the Pension Shield, you protect your spouse, preserve income, and pass on a legacy.

### A Final Word From Uncle Joe

"You can't avoid every storm, but you can choose whether you fix the roof or stand in the rain." The Shield is your roof. It's how you make sure your spouse doesn't stand in the rain when you're gone.

### Your Next Step

Don't wait until retirement day. Call for backup now. Meet with a credentialed, ethical advisor who understands pensions, insurance, and taxes. Get your Shield approved and in force — then finalize your pension election.

**Why This Conclusion Matters:** Protecting your pension isn't just about money. It's about dignity, security, and leaving a legacy. The Pension Shield Option™ isn't a tactic — it's a promise: that your pension will always protect the people you love most.

## Who Is Uncle Joe?

I dedicated my first book, *Prosperity By Design*, to my Uncle Joe—and included a short chapter of his sharp, homespun wisdom. Readers loved it. His sayings, simple but piercing, have a way of sticking with people long after they're read. My favorites are: "Done is better than perfect" and "Direction is more important than speed."

In 2018, while attending a publishing conference in Atlanta, I was trying to finalize *Stop, DROP and Roll: A Retirement Guide for First Responders.* The subject was bigger than expected, and the book needed more time. When the conference leader asked, "What else do you have?" I reached for Uncle Joe's wisdom—and wrote the first edition of *Uncle Joe's Gems* over that weekend. That little book became a tribute not just to him, but to the kind of everyday genius that too often goes unnoticed.

Uncle Joe wasn't a professor or a financial planner. He was an inspector at a circuit-breaker factory—a blue-collar man with the insight of an Ivy League economist. He could explain compound interest or dividend reinvestment with the same ease he explained how to fix a leaky faucet. When I was in second grade, he told me why utility stocks were the "paychecks that never called in sick." His lessons were never lectures; they were conversations—sometimes over coffee, sometimes while fixing my grandmother's roof together.

Money was never his problem, because he had plenty and money was never his purpose. He invested wisely, lived simply, and gave generously—of his time most of all. When someone was struggling, someone would say, "Better call Joe." He'd show up, listen, and tell a story that made the problem shrink to size. He had a way of twisting a phrase until it hit home. He also wrote out a few checks but not until he knew the real problem was fixed.

***"A friend in need, is a friend INDEED!"***

-Uncle Joe

Uncle Joe believed that wealth isn't measured in what you earn, but in what you understand. His investment ideas were clever, but his advice on living was brilliant. He showed that financial wisdom and moral clarity aren't separate subjects—they're chapters of the same book.

That spirit runs through every page of this one. The quotes you'll find from "Uncle Joe" aren't cute nostalgia; they're reminders that truth doesn't need polish, just practice. He understood life as well as money—and I hope his voice helps you do the same.

---

## About the Authors

**George McReynolds, CFP®**

George McReynolds is the Founder and Chief Executive Officer of McReynolds & Company, LLC, where he has devoted his career to helping public safety professionals and their families make confident, informed retirement decisions. A decorated U.S. Army veteran, George served as a military policeman and emergency medical technician, working in one of Europe's busiest trauma hospitals. He graduated from the Pennsylvania State Police Academy and went on to serve as a decorated police officer, including duty on one of the first SWAT teams in his county. That foundation of service shaped the way he approaches financial planning: with discipline, compassion, and an unwavering respect for those who dedicate their lives to protecting others.

As a CERTIFIED FINANCIAL PLANNER™ professional, George brings more than three decades of experience in guiding clients through the complexities of pensions, taxes, investments, and legacy planning. He has spoken at prestigious venues including Oxford University, Cambridge University, the London Stock Exchange, and the Royal Society of Medicine, as well as domestic conferences such as the FBI National Academy Association.

George is the author of *Prosperity by Design, Uncle Joe's Gems, Stop, DROP and Roll: A Retirement Guide for First*

*Responders,* and *Retire Abundantly* with Scott Keffer. His writing and speaking blend professional rigor with relatable stories, locker-room candor, and humor that makes serious financial lessons accessible. Above all, his clients know him as a caring and trusted advisor who treats their future with the same seriousness as their service to the community.

**Jim Lusk, CFP®, CLU®, ChFC®, CLF®, M.Ed.**
Jim Lusk is a nationally recognized financial educator and strategist who has taught thousands of families how to turn pensions and insurance into reliable "money machines for life." With advanced credentials including CERTIFIED FINANCIAL PLANNER™, Chartered Life Underwriter®, Chartered Financial Consultant®, Chartered Leadership Fellow®, and a master's degree in education, Jim combines technical expertise with the heart of a teacher.

He is the creator of the Private Protection Plan (PPP), a pioneering framework for replacing pension survivor options with flexible, tax-efficient protection. His insights have been shared through seminars, training programs, and his books *Die Neatly* and *Money Machines for Life.* Known for blending precision with practicality, Jim's goal has always been to help families protect income, preserve dignity, and pass on a legacy.

Together, George and Jim bring decades of service, experience, and innovation to the *Pension Shield Option*™. Their collaboration merges George's focus on first responders with Jim's national teaching legacy—delivering a proven strategy to protect your pension, your spouse, and your legacy.

---

Made in the USA
Monee, IL
13 September 2026

62981958R00059